Simon Chapman

EXPLORERS
WANTED!

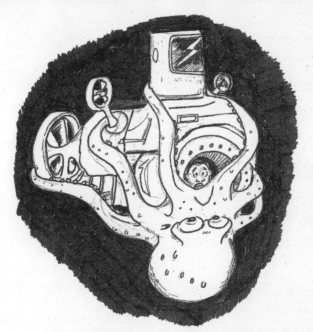

Under the Sea

EGMONT

First published in Great Britain in 2003
by Egmont Books Limited
239 Kensington High Street
London W8 6SA

Text and illustrations copyright © 2003 Simon Chapman
Cover illustration copyright © 2003 Lee Gibbons

The moral rights of the author and the cover illustrator
have been asserted

ISBN 1 4052 0554 7

10 9 8 7 6 5 4 3 2 1

A CIP catalogue record for this title
is available from the British Library

Printed and bound in Great Britain
by Mackays of Chatham Ltd, Chatham, Kent

CONTENTS

Your Mission   2

1. Skin-diving and Snorkels   11

2. SCUBA   19

3. Coral Reef   27

4. The Reef Wall   37

5. The Wreck of the
   SS Desdemona   49

6. The Open Ocean   60

7. Down into the
   Deep Abyss   75

8. The Treasure of the
   SS Desdemona   87

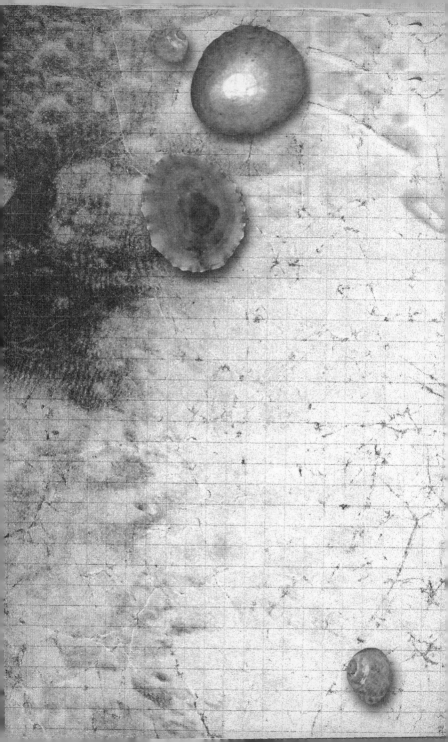

SO ... YOU WANT TO BE AN UNDERWATER EXPLORER?

Do you want to ...
Dive amongst the coral reefs ... ?

Search for **treasure** in **sunken wrecks** ... ?

Descend to the bottom of the **deepest** ocean trench?

If the answer to any of these questions is **YES**,
then this is the book for you. Read on ...

1

THIS BOOK WILL tell you how to get started – from exploring with a snorkel or **diving with a tank of air on your back,** to discovering the secrets of the deepest depths in a mini-submarine. **There are also some** pretty scary true-life stories of some of the people who have tried to explore it before ... so read on!

YOUR MISSION ...
should you choose to accept it, is to head up a diving expedition – in search of sunken treasure.

You'll be diving around the reef-fringed South Seas island of Motorua, looking for the wreck of the SS Desdemona that sank in a storm in 1909 (see expedition dossier at the end of this chapter). The island lies along a geological fault-line and its coral reefs plunge down a steep rift wall to far deeper than anyone can dive without some really special equipment. To explore the reef, the wall and its depths, you are going to need training.

Is the SS Desdemona going to be impossible to find?

What kind of treasure are you trying to find in her watery grave?

IT'S UP TO YOU TO FIND OUT.

You are going to need to learn about what you might find in the ocean, and how to survive where there is no air to breathe and thousands of tons of water pressure pushing in at you.

Time to set the scene . . .

Let's find out some vital facts about the ocean and its environment before the mission gets under way.

Seventy-one per cent of the Earth's surface is covered with water. What you find, whether it's open ocean, coral reefs, kelp forests, or deep ocean trenches, depends on where you go . . . and how deep.

Coral reefs are the tropical rainforests of the sea. This maps shows where in the world to find them.

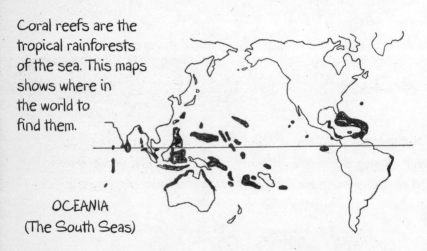

OCEANIA
(The South Seas)

Another thing you might notice under the sea, is that the water gets darker as you descend deeper. Sunlight is absorbed by any particles floating around. They take out the red and yellow colours in sunlight, allowing bluer colours to get through (sunlight is made up of all the colours of the rainbow). That's why sea water looks bluish. In the deepest parts of the ocean depths, no light gets through at all. It is pitch black. Lots of the animals that live down there have luminous markings, so that they can find others of their own kind or hunt for food.

So, what's the sea really like under the surface?
Put your head underwater and have a look.

It's wet (obviously), cold (unless, that is, you've started off
somewhere tropical), you can't breathe (also obvious), and it's
all blurry . . .

Not being able to see properly is one thing that you can do
something about straight away. Your eyes aren't designed to
work underwater, so it helps if you wear a pair of goggles.

There are a few more things to see now . . .

Wearing a good pair of goggles will make things look slightly nearer (and so bigger), than they really are . . . how big was that fish you saw? As for feeling cold and not being able to breathe, these are two things that can be avoided if you wear the right equipment. But the biggest problem you will face will be . . .

THE PRESSURE!

This doesn't mean it's going to be hard and stressful to understand all this stuff. It's just that when you dive under, you will have a huge amount of water pushing on top of you – one litre of water weighs one kilogram. Think how much weight of water you will have above you just a few metres down. Heavy, eh?

Now here comes the science!

When you are underwater, pressure pushes equally from all directions. This pressure increases the deeper down you go.

At ten metres down, there's twice the pressure there was at the surface. The air in this bottle would squash to half its size.

At 90 metres down, there's ten times the pressure. The air in the bottle would now take up a tenth of the space.

The water pressure hundreds of metres down in the ocean would crush you. What's more, going up quickly to the surface later can be a huge problem too. Gases in your blood expand as the pressure on them lessens, which can be very nasty. Many deep-sea fish puff out and burst when they are brought to the surface because of this! So would you if you held your breath at the seabed then rapidly rose to the surface.

BEFORE   AFTER

Face it, just **to survive** at all, let alone explore, you are going to have to overcome these difficulties...

· How to breathe
· How to see
· How to stay warm
· How to cope with all that pressure, man!

The Wreck of the SS Desdemona
EXPEDITION DOSSIER

In 1909, the luxury liner, SS Desdemona, went down in a storm off the South Seas island of Motorua. Despite happening so far away from Europe, the sinking was widely reported in the papers at the time, mainly because of the loss of the 'Fortune Star', a beautifully-cut diamond the size of an egg, which had been the

FORTUNE STAR

engagement present of Eva Meringue, the gorgeous actress fiancée of the millionaire industrialist, Jerry Steinburger. The couple had been about to get married on board the ship when the storm had struck. They were lucky. Their cabin had been just below the level of the main deck, and they had been amongst the first to get away on one of the liner's few lifeboats.

EVA AND JERRY

But – sadly without the diamond! That had been left in the safe of their stateroom, and so it had sunk to the seabed, along with the SS Desdemona and most of the other passengers. As for the marriage – it never took place. 'No gem, no wife,' Eva told Jerry after a passing cargo ship picked up their lifeboat. She went on to a glittering career in the movies. He kept his millions and lived the rest of his life as a virtual recluse.

The story so far . . .

Everybody knows that divers have long searched the coral reefs of Motorua and, though they have found the wrecks of several other ships which storms have dashed to pieces on the reef, they have never located the SS Desdemona.

BUT NOW YOU HAVE AN IDEA!

Just recently, this lifebelt from the SS Desdemona was washed up on the southern shore of the island.

WHAT IF . . . everybody has been looking in the **wrong** place?

WHAT IF . . . strong currents pulling along the under**sea** chasm which ru**ns** along the east side of the island, has dragge**d the** wreckage south – not north - as **everyone** had presumed?

This is the idea you recently presented to the Jerry Steinburger foundation who have given you funding for an expedition to Motorua, and promised to reward you handsomely if you can retrieve the diamond.

Just one small problem though . . .

You don't actually know how to dive!

It is obvious that you will need training. Here's how we'll do it. We'll have to start at the top and get deeper . . . and deeper.

Chapter 1
SKIN-DIVING AND SNORKELS

SKIN-DIVING IS

breathing without apparatus. The best way – the way that the pearl divers of the Tuamotus islands in Polynesia do it – is to take a deep breath, then blow all the air out of their lungs and dive. It's all about buoyancy. You need oxygen to make your muscles work, but if you take down a whole lung-full of air, it'll make you float back up again. Ever tried pushing an inflatable ball underwater? It's exactly like that. When the pearl divers breathe out before they go underwater, the oxygen from their breath has passed into their bloodstream, but they don't have a ribcage full of air to keep pulling them back up to the surface while they are trying to swim down. With practice, experienced pearl divers can manage one-and-a-half minutes underwater, more than this if they don't dive as deep.

At the huge depths the pearl divers dive to, the water pressure pushes their goggles against their eyes and squashes their lips and cheeks right in.

Really fit divers can get down to around forty metres - that's the same as the height of a twelve-storey building - but ten metres is about as deep as most people can go. At this depth, your ears 'pop' - the pressure of all that water pressing in on you pushes your eardrums in slightly - it's uncomfortable, but not really harmful as long as you equalise the pressure inside with the pressure outside by pinching your nose and blowing out. (If you don't, you can burst your eardrums inwards!)

GETTING KITTED OUT

Let's face it - hardly any of us would be able to dive as deep as an experienced pearl diver, but there are certain pieces of simple equipment that can make you swim faster and see better while you are underwater.

MASK: This is essential otherwise everything will be blurred when you are beneath the waves.

SNORKEL: This allows you to remain face down when you are swimming on the surface, looking at what's going on underneath while you continue to breathe. When you dive, remember to have just enough breath left in your lungs to blow out the water when you resurface. Otherwise you'll swallow it all!

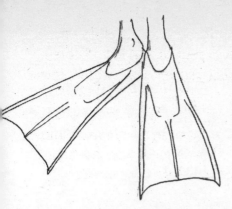

FINS: Flippers can certainly help you to move faster and deeper through the water.

OUR SNORKELLER...

sees something ahead of **her** – a minuscule **tiddler** (the fish, I mean)

'It was this big.'

How did she get it so wrong?

A. The diver is a liar.

B. The diver is deluded.

C. It was one of those weird light effects.

Answer on page 14

C. The light rays from the fish refract (bend) when they travel from the water to the air inside the mask. The rays enter the eye at a wide angle which makes the fish appear as if it is much closer, and so larger, than it really is.

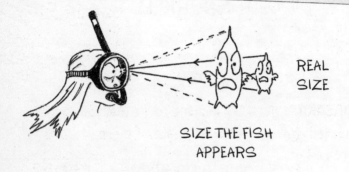

REAL SIZE

SIZE THE FISH APPEARS

BE AWARE!

Now you are kitted out, here are some of the dangers which snorkellers should look out for whilst swimming.

1. **SEA URCHINS**: Don't touch! The spines break off and work their way in deeper. PAINFUL!

2. **CORAL**: Don't touch either! The tiny animals (polyps) under the hard surface sting and can get into cuts which take a long time to heal.

3. **JELLYFISH**: Nasty little stingers. In Australia, the sting of the box jellyfish can be lethal. You can become paralysed and then drown. Many beaches have kits with special anti-venom in case this happens to swimmers.

4. **SPEEDBOATS**: Unfortunately, people do get run over by them while swimming. Nasty propellers. However, as sound travels better - and further - in water than in air, you can usually hear them coming.

5. **BREAKING WAVES**: Indicate rocks that you can be dashed against. Particularly nasty if there are sea urchins around the rocks (don't become a human in cushion).

For exploring the shallow water around the coasts, snorkelling is ideal. No expensive equipment and no training is needed and you can still experience some incredible underwater sights. But what if you want to go deeper? You could use a really long snorkel tube up to the surface and strap on some heavy weights to stop you floating back up. However, the problem is that, lower than half-a-metre or so, this doesn't work. It's that pressure thing again! Human lungs can't suck air down a tube very far, especially if they've got a weight of water pressing them in. To get the air down to the diver, you need a pump.

IMPROVISING EQUIPMENT

In the 1920s, an English marine biologist called John Kitching used to explore the kelp forest off Devon in a helmet made from an upside-down milk churn with a window put in it! Friends on the surface took turns pumping air to him through a garden hose, using a foot pump. John wandered through the kelp (which is basically enormous seaweed), with lead weights tied around him to keep him down, and a pair of garden shears to snip off samples.

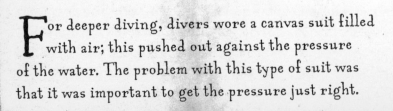

For deeper diving, divers wore a canvas suit filled with air; this pushed out against the pressure of the water. The problem with this type of suit was that it was important to get the pressure just right.

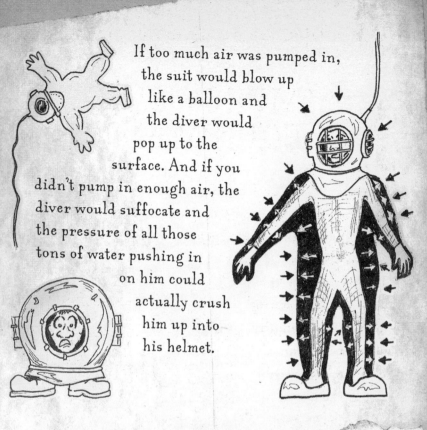

If too much air was pumped in, the suit would blow up like a balloon and the diver would pop up to the surface. And if you didn't pump in enough air, the diver would suffocate and the pressure of all those tons of water pushing in on him could actually crush him up into his helmet.

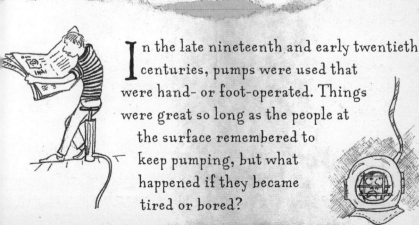

In the late nineteenth and early twentieth centuries, pumps were used that were hand- or foot-operated. Things were great so long as the people at the surface remembered to keep pumping, but what happened if they became tired or bored?

Eventually, all these problems were solved with the invention of reliable motor pumps. For some longer dives, air lines to pumps on the surface are still used. But it's not very convenient...and it isn't very cheap.

The ideal thing, of course, would be to carry your own supply of air with you. Here's one way that people used to do it.

The sponge divers of the Mediterranean (they dived for sponges – they weren't sponge themselves!), used to carry up-ended jars as they swam to the bottom of the sea. Provided the jar stayed with its mouth facing downwards, the air in it would float up and stay inside. All a diver had to do was to put their mouth to the edge of the jar, tip it slightly and suck in a breath of air.

But is this really practical? Well, no, not really! What you need is a strap-on tank of air. We're talking about **Self-Contained Underwater Breathing Apparatus** here – or **SCUBA** equipment to you and me. It's time to get technical.

Chapter 2
SCUBA

YOUR DESTINATION, THE South Seas island of Motorua is surrounded by coral reefs. The SS Desdemona hit one of these before sinking into the deeper water around the edges of the reef. There is no way around it, you will need dive training if you are to complete your mission.

EQUIPMENT CHECKLIST

This is a list of the equipment a modern SCUBA-diver needs.

The key to it all is some really fancy kit - and the training to use it all PROPERLY and SAFELY.

- **AQUALUNG**: To give you a steady supply of air.
- **WET SUIT**: You'll need to keep warm unless you are diving in shallow, tropical waters. Wet suits are made of a rubbery, plastic material called neoprene. They're designed to insulate you - and keep your body heat in, even though they get wet.
- **REGULATOR**: A valve that lets you breathe air from the aqualung when you need it. The air you breathe is at the same pressure as the water around you which means it pushes your lungs out with an equal force to the force of the water around you.

- **WEIGHT BELT**: A belt which you can slot weights on to to make you heavier in the water.

- **BUOYANCY CONTROL DEVICE (BCD)**: It looks a bit like a life jacket. If you fill it with air (from your tank), you float up. If you empty it, you sink. You control the amount of air in your BCD to determine at what level you 'float' in the water.

- **DIVE CONSOLE/DIVE COMPUTER**: This tells you vital information you need to know, like how deep you are, how much air there is left in your tank, and how quickly you can safely come up to the surface without having 'pressure problems'.

ALSO OPTIONAL . . .

- **WATCH**: You need to know how long you've been underwater and how much longer your air will last.
- **COMPASS**: It's all too easy to lose your way, especially in dark murky water.
- **KNIFE**: If you get tangled up, you will need to free yourself.
- **DIVE LIGHT**: Essential for peering into nooks and crannies.
- **HOOD**: Your body can lose a lot of heat from your head, so in deep or cold water, keep it warm.

A DIVER'S KIT

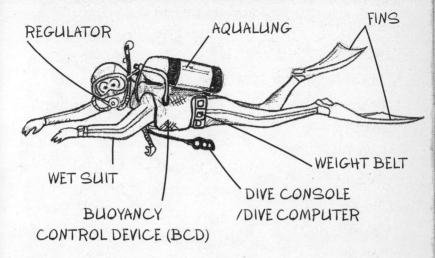

REGULATOR

AQUALUNG

FINS

WEIGHT BELT

WET SUIT

DIVE CONSOLE
/DIVE COMPUTER

BUOYANCY
CONTROL DEVICE (BCD)

And last, but not least, you need a BUDDY! - someone to dive with. The two of you can look out for each other if there are ever any problems.

REMEMBER

Never go diving without a buddy who can look out for you in case things go wrong.

The trouble is . . . you've got Jack - Jack Custard. He's all you could get at short notice, the only person you could find who had the time (and the money) to go gallivanting off to the South Sea Islands on one of your hair-brained schemes. 'Two valves short of a regulator' he may be, but he's all there is!

Now to start your dive training. Here are some of the things you'll learn.

1. **How to set up your kit**
   - How to fit your breathing tube with its regulator valves on to your aqualung.

2. **Sign language** - Here are some of the hand signals you will need to learn initially.

Make a fist and hold it out

A. 'LOW ON AIR'

B. 'DANGER'

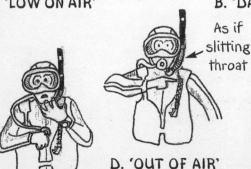

As if slitting throat

D. 'OUT OF AIR'

C. 'BUDDY BREATHE'

E. 'LET'S GO UP'

3. **Information about pressure** – Planning how far down you will go, and how long you will spend down there so you don't have problems coming up.

4. **Safety drill** – Knowing when and where it's safe to dive, and what to do if you have a problem while you are down there.

Now let's see what you can remember. After all, in your dive training you would have to pass a test. Of course you'll need a few practice dives – maybe test out the gear somewhere safe like a swimming pool before you start your scuba-diving for real.

What do these pieces of equipment do?

Match the number of the kit item below with the letter on the next page.

1. Buoyancy Control Device
2. Dive console
3. Wet suit
4. Snorkel
5. Regulator
6. Weight belt

A. Helps you go up and down by filling up with, or letting out, air.

B. Keeps you down.

C. Use it at the surface so that you don't waste air from your aqualung.

D. Gives you information on how deep you are and how much air is left in your tank.

E. Supplies air on demand as you breathe in. The air is at the same pressure as the surrounding water.

F. You need this if you dive in cold water.

Answers are on page 26

YOUR AIR SUPPY

You get 30-50 minutes per tank - how long your supply lasts depends on how quickly you breathe and how deep you go. The deeper you go, the more the air is squashed up (high pressure), and the more you use up. When your air supply runs low, you have to come up. An aqualung works fine to about 50 metres depth, then there are problems . . . yes, the pressure again!

Pure oxygen, the gas that you need to breathe, becomes poisonous under pressure. Strangely, it also smells of stale ginger beer. The first effects of oxygen poisoning is that the diver feels drunk. Roughly the same thing happens with the nitrogen gas that makes up nearly 80% of air (this is called nitrogen narcosis).

To solve the problems that oxygen and nitrogen can give you, and another deep pressure problem called 'the bends' which we will investigate later on, deep divers sometimes use a mixture of oxygen and helium in their air tank. Yes, helium is the gas that they put in balloons to make them float and the same gas that makes your voice go squeaky if you breathe it in. If divers could speak through their mouthpieces, they would sound like Mickey Mouse.

What if you want to go deeper?

You need to get very technical indeed. Even breathing special exotic mixtures of gases with oxygen, scuba-divers can't dive much deeper than a hundred metres or so. The human body is just not designed to withstand that much pressure. One way to get around this problem is to wear a fully-covering, armoured pressure suit.

So, that's your training done for the moment. As long as you remember your training and remain safe, your dives will go smoothly. Did you get most of the questions right?

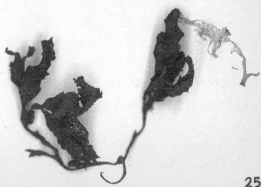

You've got your tank, wet suit, and other equipment so you can start to try and find the wreck of the SS Desdemona. You've found a buddy to dive with and you've managed to hire a boat that can take you to the area where you think the shipwreck has ended up. There are quite a few places it could be. It's better to do some practice dives first, then dive shallow and explore the eastern reef first, before you set off down the reef wall towards the shelf above the ocean trench.

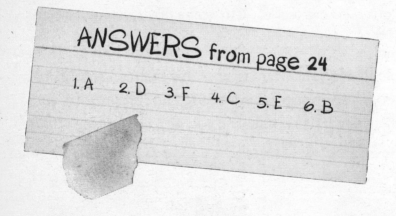

ANSWERS from page 24

1. A   2. D   3. F   4. C   5. E   6. B

Chapter 3
CORAL REEF

YOUR FIRST SCUBA-dive is going to be around the coral reef that fringes Motorua island. The reef juts out around the island. Most of it's around ten metres deep, but some bits jut up above the water when the tide is low. It was on one of these outcrops that the SS Desdemona probably ripped its hull open all those years ago. You and your buddy are equipped with wet suits, air tanks, BCDs, and everything else you might need. This is an 'exploratory dive' – a chance to get an idea of what the reef is like and work out some ideas about where you think the shipwreck may have ended up.

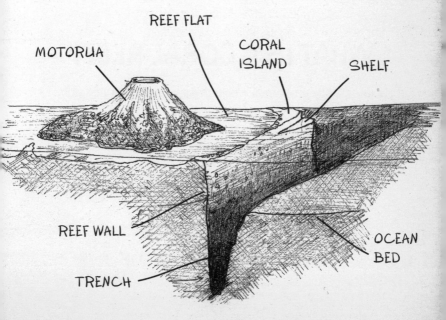

MOTORUA · REEF FLAT · CORAL ISLAND · SHELF · REEF WALL · TRENCH · OCEAN BED

You prepare for your dive and jump off the boat. The shallow water is sunlit and clear. You can see the knobbly tree-like outlines of the corals of the reef, as well as fish - angel fish, clown fish, parrot fish - that are shoaling in their thousands. This is the rainforest of the ocean and the place is teaming with life!

WHAT IS A CORAL REEF?

Coral is actually an animal - or rather a community of tiny jellyfish-like animals called polyps, none bigger than the size of your fingernail.

JELLYFISH - Turn him upside down . . .

Encase him in limestone . . .
and he becomes CORAL POLYP

Polyp communities grow up into a fantastic variety of shapes; stag horns, fans, feathers . . . and even brains! But forget that corals look like they should be plants. Those structures can be rock hard; the polyps remove chemicals from the seawater and surround themselves with limestone for

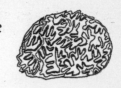

protection. Some of the harder ones live in partnership with simple microscopic plants. The polyps provide the plants with carbon dioxide which the plants need to make food for themslevs by photosynthesis and in return the plants provide oxygen and food substances which the polyps need. Some of the carbon dioxide is also used to make the limestone casing for the coral.

BRAIN CORAL

STAG HORN CORAL

SEA FAN

Hard corals, growing in shallow warm seas in the tropics build up into reefs around tropical islands. In fact many of these islands are themselves the remains of coral reefs that have been built up over the years with debris and coral sand.

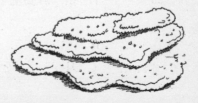

PIPE ORGAN CORAL

STONEY COLONIAL CORAL

DID YOU KNOW?

One of the biggest dangers to the barrier reef are
the 'crown of thorns' starfish which multiply
in huge numbers and scrunch their way
through the living coral. Few creatures
will eat them as they are
quite poisonous.

DID YOU KNOW?

The Australian barrier reef which stretches in a line
2,000 kilometres long down the north-eastern side of
Australia, by itself makes up three per cent of the
world's coral reefs. It is so big, it can be seen from
outer space.

GREAT
BARRIER REEF

Coral reefs support a huge variety of sea creatures. Each has its own job to do in the reef community.

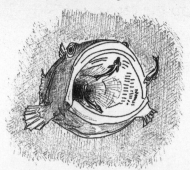

PERSONAL GROOMING
- cleaner wrasse pick the scraps off the teeth of a grumpy grouper.

GROUPER AND CLEANER WRASSE

STREET SWEEPERS - crabs and prawns that
scuttle about disposing of any wast

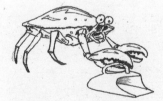

CRAB CLEANER

SHRIMP STREET SWEEPER

SHOPPERS - Angel
fish, parrot fish, and clown fish nibble away at the coral polyps, seeking out bargains and tasty morsels.

Stag Horn Coral £2.99

SALE

SEA FAN

VENTILATION - a sea fan (actually a soft type of coral).

MUSICIANS - there is a coral reef jazz ensemble - trumpet fish, pipe fish, guitar fish, and saxophone fish.

GUITAR FISH

Actually, one of the fish in the jazz band is made up.

There's no such thing as a saxophone fish, silly!

TRIGGER FISH

While we're on the subject of sea creatures with silly names, how about this for a gang of desperadoes? - the cutlass fish, hatchet fish, trigger fish, and pistol shrimp.

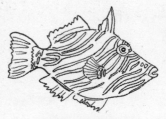

PISTOL SHRIMP

Pistol shrimps have a unique way of catching their prey. They click their claws with such force that the shockwave stuns their prey - a bit like knocking someone out by clicking your fingers.

HAZARDS: Danger on the Reef

With so many fish about, you would expect a few predators around, maybe a barracuda or even a shark or two. But you might be surprised about which animals are the truly dangerous ones. Match the following weapon to the animals as shown below.

WHICH ANIMAL . . .

A. Has a deadly spike?   **B.** Has a painful spike?

C. Has a deadly bite?   **D.** Has a deadly bite, but is more likely to slither away?

E. Is painful to tread on?   **F.** Is deadly to tread on?

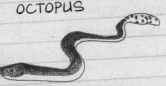

1. STONE FISH

2. CONE SHELL

3. BLUE-RINGED OCTOPUS

4. TOAD FISH

5. SEA SNAKE

6. ZEBRA FISH

Answers on page 34

I haven't even mentioned Giant clams yet!

In some old films some poor victim was always getting their leg clamped in a giant clam, squirming until his or her air has almost run out, at which point the hero comes swimming in, prizes the sides of the shell apart and makes a fantastic rescue. Actually that's one of those myths that is just not true. The unexciting truth is giant clams just don't move that quickly. You'd have to leave your foot in there for a long time before it finally got the hint and slowly closed the sides together.

Hazards: ANSWERS from page 33

1. **STONE FISH** – F – Sad but true.

2. **CONE SHELL** – A – Vicious little brutes. They have a poisonous harpoon-like organ that can whip out from the pointed end of the shell and spike someone picking the shell up.

3. **BLUE-RINGED OCTOPUS** – C – These are tiny, but their spit is so poisonous it can cause death in minutes.

4. **TOAD FISH** – E – Beware the nasty spines along its back.

5. **SEA SNAKE** – D – Sea snakes are the most deadly snakes in the world – 20 times as poisonous as a cobra with enough venom to kill you several times over.

6. **ZEBRA FISH** – B – The spines have grooves which the fish's venom is pumped down. How bad your wound is would depend on how many times you were spiked.

Also, there are fire corals, fire sponges (not one to use in your bath), sea anemones, and lots of other nasties that can sting you. So, overall, it's best NEVER to touch . . . not least because you'd be damaging the creatures of the reef. Whenever you touch a coral or a sponge, you remove some of the protective mucous slime that it keeps around itself to prevent infection. Also, if you are not careful, you might accidentally break bits off and graze or cut your skin. If you do accidentally hurt yourself, seek treatment and clean the wound immediately.

People are far more damaging to the reef, generally, than its inhabitants are to people. Some reefs are over-fished, sometimes by dynamiting the reef to quickly kill lots of fish. Of course, the fishermen can only do this a couple of times before the reef is ruined and there is nothing more to catch. Even divers who come to see the reef often damage it. Anchors from their boats drag over the fragile coral. Like rainforests on land, coral reefs are threatened by mans' activities. They need looking after and preserving.

Remember your buddy? That's the friend who's partnered up with you for safety on this dive. Jack taps you on the shoulder, points out the blue-ringed octopus that you were just centimetres away from brushing past. He makes this signal.

What do you think it means?
A. Buddy breathe
B. Let's go up
C. Out of air
D. Low on air
E. Danger   Answers on page 36

ANSWER from page 35

D. Low on air.

A.   B.   C.   D.   E.

You check your air gauge and think you ought to go to the surface while you both still have enough air.

Which of the signals shown above do you think you should make?   Answer on page 38

Now think back to your training. Your ascent should be controlled and slow. Let some air from your tank into your BCD to help you rise. Turn around slowly while you are going up so you can see where you are and hold one hand above your head, just in case you knock into anything overhead.

You can feel a current pulling you slightly out to sea as you ascend. Below, you can see the darker, deeper water where the reef flat ends and the wall begins. Anything sinking – like a ship, you think – might be pulled over the edge by that current. Going down there, you decide, will have to be your next dive. Right now, you are low on air and you must go up. Slowly though. Remember, you don't want to have problems as the pressure lessens. When you arrive at the surface, you inflate your BCD like a life jacket and wait for your dive boat to pick you up.

Chapter 4
THE REEF WALL

YOUR NEXT DIVE is going to be down the wall of the fore reef – where the waves from the open sea hit the reef. The water is rougher on the surface than on your last dive, and there are underwater currents that may drag you up or down without warning. These currents also bring nutrients which the coral polyps feed on. The wall is the part of the reef where there is the most variety of living things. Think of it like a tower block. The nicest flats, with the most sunlight, are at the top. As you go down, you'll see different sorts of coral branching out from the sides like purple sea fans waving in the current – if you look at them closely, you might see the tiny tentacles of the polyps reaching out to get at the nutrients floating past.

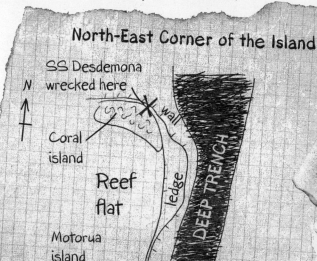

North-East Corner of the Island

N

SS Desdemona wrecked here

Coral island

Reef flat

Motorua island

wall

ledge

DEEP TRENCH

Don't get too close though. The polyps sting. Further down, at the bottom of the wall, it will be shady. There are no plants living with the corals that can use the sunlight. The corals here will be flimsier and there will be lots of sponges which filter the water for their nutrients. Here, too, are caves where the meanest, grumpiest residents of the coral reef live.

Be prepared – and remember to keep an eye on your watch, your air gauge, your pressure gauge, and your buddy too! Once in the water, the first thing you and your buddy will have to do is sink.

1. Which bit of apparatus will help you do this?

2. What do you have to do with it?

3. If the current pulls you down too quickly, what could you do with it?

4. If you had to rise quickly, what bit of kit could you get rid of?

Your choices are . . .

A. Let some air out

B. Let some air in

C. Buoyancy Control Device (BCD)

D. Weight belt

Answers on page 45

You slowly sink down alongside the wall, kicking occasionally with your flippers to stop the current swirling you around and taking you too much to one side. You see . . .

Clown fish nestling for protection in amongst the stinging tentacles of a sea anemone (they are immune to its stings.)

A green turtle biting chunks out of a jellyfish.

A moray eel poking its head out from a crack in the coral rock. These have sharp teeth and can be dangerous. The mouth keeps on opening like that at you not because the eel is about to attack but because it has to keep water passing over its gills. At some dive sites, there are moray eels that are used to divers and let them pat their noses. But would you really like to try it?

For a second or two, the light above you is blocked out as a huge manta ray 'flies' on its outstretched wings, passing not even two metres above your head. Attached to its belly are two remoras which have hitched a lift using special, ridged sucker pads on their heads.

Manta rays are harmless. All they eat are the near microscopic plant and animal plankton that drifts everywhere in the sea. It hoovers them up into its gaping mouth.

Shortly after the distraction caused by the manta ray, you notice some other large shapes in the murky water beyond the reef wall . . .

SHARKS!

What do you do?

- Swim like hell back to the boat?
- Dive deeper?
- Ignore them?
- Stay still?
- Swim towards them to get a closer look?

DON'T PANIC.
You have to assess the danger. What type of sharks are they? Are you bleeding? Is there anything bleeding near you? In reality, despite their fearsome reputation, much of their aggressiveness is just hype. You know how it is. People fix on something dangerous and then spice up the stories with lots of juicy, gory bits to make your stomach turn and make you really listen.

OK, some of the hype is true. Some sharks do attack people, but when mathematicians have looked at just how many attacks there are, this is what they worked out . . .

- Only 12 out of the 350 types of shark have ever actually attacked people.
- You are twice as likely to be hit by lightning than be attacked by a shark.
- You are 3,000 times as likely to be hit by another car as you drive to the seaside than suffer a shark attack.

The sharks probably won't be too bothered by you. You are not something they usually eat. But, just for your peace of mind, the most dangerous are Bull, Tiger, Oceanic White Tip and the Great White – and these last two are more often found in cool, open ocean.

What do you know about sharks?

True or False?

1. All sharks are predators – they chase and hunt fish and other live prey?

2. The Great White is the most dangerous type?

3. All sharks are fairly big for fish – man-sized or bigger?

4. Sharks are the fastest swimming fish in the ocean?

5. Sharks can detect minute quantities of blood in the water; this helps them hunt down their prey?

6. Sharks don't just have five senses like us (sight, hearing, smell, taste, touch); they have a sixth sense too?

7. Sharks can't control their buoyancy like most other fish; they have to keep swimming otherwise they sink?

8. Sharks are caught by fishermen who cut off their fins and throw them back in the water?

Answers on page 42-43

DID YOU KNOW?

Thresher sharks use their long fins to thrash around wildly in the middle of shoals of fish to confuse and daze them. They have also been seen using their tails to stun unsuspecting sea birds floating on the surface of the water!

ANSWERS from page 41

1. **FALSE.** Gigantic whale sharks (fifteen metres) and basking sharks (ten metres), trawl through the sea with their gigantic mouths open, eating nothing bigger than plankton (near-microscopic animals) which they sieve out much the same way as some whales do. Some sharks, like the Wobbegong, spend their time on the seabed scrunching shellfish – a much easier and relaxed way of life than hunting fast-moving fish.

2. **TRUE.** But you're probably not likely to be in a situation where a Great White would attack you. At up to six metres or so long and weighing a tonne, the Great White is the biggest and most dangerous shark. They live in cool water in the open oceans and feed on prey like sealions. Great Whites are rare and you would be very unlikely to come across one unless you went looking for it. The dangerous sharks that divers come across more often are Bull sharks and Tiger sharks. These can become excited and dangerous if people throw bait (like meat or dead fish) to attract them. Even so, they are normally unlikely to attack.

3. **FALSE**. The smallest type is the Spined Pygmy shark – only 15 centimetres when fully grown. Another mini-shark, the Cookie Cutter shark, is only 40 centimetres long and has jaws a bit like a circular biscuit cutter. It latches itself onto the side of its prey, usually another shark, and bores out a chunk of skin and flesh to eat, then detaches itself and swims off. Nice!

4. **FALSE**. Tuna and Sailfish (amongst others) are faster.

5. **TRUE**. Some sharks can detect blood from a wounded animal 500 metres away – if the water current is travelling in the right direction. Hammerhead sharks have their nostrils widely spaced, so they can home in on the scent of their prey with greater accuracy.

6. **TRUE**. All sharks can detect electrical impulses from the nervous systems of their prey. This helps when hunting at night or in cloudy water.

7. **TRUE**. A shark's side-fins are like little wings. Unlike other fish, sharks' bodies do not contain a bag of air called a swim bladder – a bit like a Buoyancy Control Device. Sharks have to keep swimming forward to generate lift force to stop themselves sinking.

8. **TRUE**. Sadly, thousands of sharks die like this each year. This is because the fins are used to make a delicacy called 'shark's fin soup'.

The sad fact is that, in general, sharks have a bad press. They are predators – top of the food chain – but the number of people actually attacked by sharks is minuscule. Sharks have much better things to eat – like fish . . . other sharks . . . cans, bottles, clothes, shoes, half a crocodile, undetonated explosives! Yes, all these things have been found in the bellies of sharks that have been caught. Humans are far more dangerous to sharks than they are to us.

Ignoring the sharks, you continue down the coral tower block. You've left the hard coral of the reef flat behind now. Here, there are soft whip corals and sea fans in reds, pinks, and purples, that waft around in the slight up current, and long, tubular sponges sticking out from the rock wall. Fewer fish are to be seen – there's less food to live on. The wall carries on downwards into blackness.

Parts of the wall cut in backwards. There are overhangs and caves with coral growing down from the ceiling. You glimpse a spiny lobster. It waves its feelers at you, then scuttles back into cover.

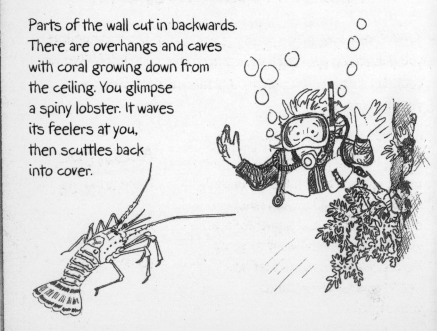

As you swim along, you feel the current buffeting you around and you feel yourself being tugged down slightly. You're being swept along the edge of the wall and you have to stop your descent. Now! Your depth gauge reads twenty-seven metres and that's lower than you intended to go. You let some air into your BCD and kick up with your fins. Neutral buoyancy again. You're not sinking any more, but the current is still pushing you along the cliff edge, and there's some coral sticking out ahead of you. It looks like knobbly deer antlers - is it stag horn coral?

You're going to hit it!

You kick against the current, and desperately twist your body to avoid a collision.

Missed . . . but thwack!

You hit rock. You hear it scraping along your aqualung and, as you push away, you catch your arm on the coral. OW! Part of your wet suit sleeve is ripped and there's a nasty graze on your forearm.

You're breathing deeply. Too deeply. Being this deep down, you'll be using up your air too fast. Your air supply is getting low. You must start coming up. You signal to Jack, your buddy, that you want to go up. He communicates back that he sees you and understands your signal.

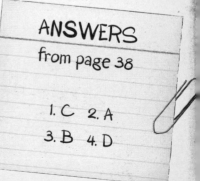

ANSWERS
from page 38

1. C 2. A
3. B 4. D

45

You rise slowly, trying to rise a metre every three seconds (not always easy in the current). You hold one hand above your head to make sure you don't hit anything, and you turn slowly and look around as you go up. You make it to twenty metres depth, but all that exertion so far down earlier on has meant you are close to running out of air. You can't just hold your breath and swim up from here. The air in your lungs would expand as the pressure outside lessened. Your lungs would burst. You will need to breath some of Jack's air. Many divers are equipped with a spare regulator mouthpiece just in case this happens. However, Jack is not! You will need to take turns breathing from the mouthpiece that Jack is using. This is called buddy breathing.

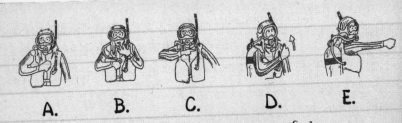

A.   B.   C.   D.   E.

1. Hand signal to Jack that you are out of air. **Which signal is it?**

2. Now, hand signal to Jack that you need to buddy breathe. **Which signal is it?**

Answers on page 48.

You carry on slowly going up, taking turns to breathe from his regulator. When you get to a depth of five metres, you stop and wait for three minutes. This is called a safety stop. Yes – you guessed it. It's all to do with those pressure problems again. It's to make sure you don't get 'the bends'.

So what would happen if you did go up too fast? And what does 'the bends' mean?

It's not what you are thinking . . . the divers don't actually bend! In the high pressure under the sea, nitrogen gas, which makes up most of the air that you breathe, dissolves in your blood. When you start coming up to the surface again, the nitrogen forms into bubbles of gas inside your muscles. This can be very painful and if the bubbles form inside your nervous system – the spine or the brain – the diver can lose consciousness, become paralysed, or even die. Deep-sea divers have to come up to the surface in slow stages, stopping for rests to decompress and allowing the nitrogen bubbles to disappear before they come up completely.

Once your safety stop is over, you and Jack swim up to the surface, inflate your BCDs like life jackets, and wait for your boat to pick you up. You notice that the current has taken you quite some distance south-eastwards (you check your compass) from where you started your dive. That has taught you something important. You may not have found the wreck of the SS Desdemona on this dive but you now have a pretty good idea of where to look. The ship broke up on the reef roughly where you set off from today. If it sank down the wall, the chances are that what was left of it floated in the same direction as you did. If you look at some undersea charts, you might be able to work out where to plan your next dive.

ANSWERS from page 46

1. C - 'Out of Air'

2. B - 'Buddy Breathe'

C.   B.

Chapter 5
THE WRECK OF THE SS DESDEMONA

UNDERSEA CURRENTS! THAT'S the key to what happened to the wreck of the SS Desdemona . . . and the treasure that it holds. When you dived down the reef wall, you were swept North-East. What if the same thing happened to the wrecked ship?

Back on Motorua, you have a good look at a deep-sea chart that you managed to acquire before you set off on this expedition. This shows a ledge off the north-eastern part of the reef wall. The ledge is only fifty metres down and it might be worth checking out. You won't be the first to try there. The rusted hull of a ship was found in that area several years ago by an oceanographic survey team, but apart from stating that the wreckage was coated in coral and home to a particularly large octopus, the scientists' report wasn't particularly interesting. It did say, though, that the ship probably wasn't the SS Desdemona, as it didn't seem large enough. However, the scientists added that they didn't spend long on their dive because it was difficult to control their mini-sub in the strong undersea currents.

DIVE PLAN

To do this dive, you have had to have extra training with a skilled instructor. This will be a deeper dive than before, so you needed to know even more about how to make decompression stops (to avoid getting 'the bends'), when you resurface. Also, inside the shipwreck is what divers call an 'overhead environment' and you have to be taught how to deal with that. You will be in a closed-in space and, if things go wrong, you can't just float to the surface.

Underwater Archaeology

Luckily for you, finding this wreck will not be too difficult. According to the oceanographers, the hull had not become totally covered in silt over the years – probably because of the fast-flowing currents washing over it. Many shipwrecks become covered in sediment as time passes, and being covered up is what keeps them preserved. Spanish galleons from 500 years ago and Roman galleys, 2,000 years old, have survived without rotting because silt smothers the wooden hulls and stops oxygen getting in and living things eating (or rotting) them away. Any wood not covered up rots within a few years. Metals, though, often survive. Quite often, metal objects corrode or rust on the outside and then these concrete-hard layers, known as 'concretions', protect what's left inside.

Can you guess what is inside each of these?

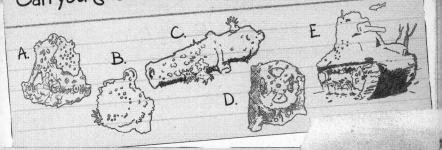

A.

B.

C.

D.

E.

ANSWERS

A. **BRASS SEXTANT**: A device for measuring latitude (horizontal position), by sighting the position of the stars above the horizon.

B. **CHRONOMETER** (watch): This one was excavated by divers off the coast of Jamaica. Much of the town of Port Royal had slid into the sea during an earthquake in 1692. An X-ray of the watch showed that it stopped at 11.43am to be precise.

C. **CANNONS**: Cannons and metal anchors are often the most obvious signs of a wreck.

D. **GEAR WHEELS**: This was part of a device that showed the motion of the planets around the sun. It was found off the Greek Island of Antikythera and dated back to 30 B.C. This was an incredibly important find, as it showed that the Ancient Greeks had far more complicated technology than was previously thought.

E. **LIGHT TANK**: (Japanese) from the Chuuk lagoon in the South Pacific, on one of a fleet of more than sixty ships that the Americans sank there during WWII.

In the Mediterranean, divers have brought up thousands of amphorae (storage pots) from Greek and Roman ships. Often the contents have decayed completely (they make excellent homes for octopus who think that the pots are like cosy little caves) but, once in a while, enough have survived so that scientists can analyse what they contained, for example, wine, olive oil or grain. Around 1950, the famous French diver, Jacques Cousteau, recovered an amphora of 2,000-year-old Roman wine which was still sealed. In front of a press conference, he drank the wine; it was still fresh! Unfortunately, he didn't think to have any of it analysed! No one has found another amphora of Roman wine since.

Jacques had problems removing all the silt which had preserved the wrecks he was excavating. His solution was to use a sort of gigantic vacuum cleaner to suck it up. Unfortunately, one time, it also sucked up much of a ship full of delicate Roman plates and smashed them to pieces. One of his friends, Frederic Dumas, tried excavating a shipwreck using a pneumatic drill – but that just bounced him three metres off the bottom of the sea. And, when Jacques and Frederic recovered un-smashed pieces of crockery, they would stick price labels on them and

52

show it to the archaeologists on their ship above, who were watching on close circuit TV, joking that they would smash the plates unless the archaeologists paid up quickly. Underwater archaeology has come a long way since those early days.

Wrecks are now mapped out and the silt is carefully taken away. Anything made of natural substances, like wood, is carefully packaged and often treated with chemicals to stop it disintegrating when it is brought to the surface.

Your motor boat takes you some way out into the open sea beyond the reef wall and, once again, you and your buddy jump into the water, release the air from your BCD and begin your descent.

You soon find the front section of the hull. The wreck is like a mini reef. Soft, pink corals have grown over much of the hull and fish teem in huge shoals. There are predators too. Keep a look out for Bull sharks skulking around, ready to dash in and snatch unsuspecting fish. You switch your dive light on and enter through a great gash in the side, where the ship split when it hit the seabed all those years ago.

You look around you! A corridor leads off...

There are pipes along the corridor. Do not touch them! They are encrusted with razor clams which will easily slice into your hands or cut your air tubes. There are several doorways off the corridor, opening into dark cabins cluttered with floating debris that might once have been bits of furniture. In one room, you disturb several small fish which dart out of an open porthole. In another, something long and snake-like is  illuminated in your torch beam for an instant as it slithers through a hole in the floor. It's very creepy. In these still, black surroundings, the hiss of your breathing, and the sound of the bubbles coming out of your regulator, seem especially loud. You reach a larger room at the front of the wreck. It's lighter in here. The windows have long since broken and fish now mill in and out of the rough, square holes. You find a coral-encrusted telephone, half hanging off a rusted metal panel with several broken dials and buttons. Maybe this was a navigation room.

You use your knife to chip away at the corrosion on one of the panels ... and uncover the words 'Liverpool, England'. This ship, you think, could be the SS Desdemona. It was built in Liverpool. Maybe ... but no ... this ship is far too small.

Suddenly, there is movement in the shadows. Something is snaking out to touch you - a long, boneless arm with suckers down its length!

You turn around to face . . . **an octopus!**

It's big! Each arm is about a metre-and-a-half long.

What are your reactions?

Answer these questions to test your octopus knowledge.

1. **The octopus is probably . . .**

A. Curious?

B. Hungry and out to eat you?

C. Attracted to your scent?

2. **If it attacked you, the thing you would most want to avoid would be . . .**

A. An over-friendly hug from its powerful tentacles?

B. A nasty nip from its beak-like mouth?

C. Getting stuck to its suckers?

3. **If the octopus is scared of you, it might . . .**

A. Shoot out an octopus-sized squirt of ink?

B. Shoot out a jet of water to propel itself backwards?

C. Squeeze out of the fist-sized hole in the corner of the cabin wall?

Answers on pages 56-57

1. A - **Curious** is most likely. Octopus are the most intelligent invertebrate (animal without a backbone). Scientists have set octopus tasks like opening bottles to get at food inside them - which they always manage.

2. B - **A nasty nip**. The beak-like mouth is the only hard part of an octopus and can give you a nasty bite. Octopus saliva is poisonous and liquifies flesh, so that the octopus can easily suck out its food. You don't need to worry that much about the strong grip. If you can keep it wrestling (but stay out of the way of its jaws!), it will tire out quickly. As for the suckers, they can hold on to surfaces like rocks so tightly that, sometimes, they have been left behind when an octopus has been pulled off. They might cause you some damage but very little compared to what the beak would do! And octopus have been known to bite divers.

3. A, B, and C - **All three are possible**.

A frightened octopus will squirt out ink so that a predator confuses this for the octopus and attacks it. And if one of their arms is held by an attacker, they will sacrifice it in order to get away. They can always grow another one later. Octopus do travel by jet propulsion in this way, and can squeeze through tiny holes. Even their eyes can be squashed when necessary. The only part that can't be squashed is the horny mouth.

DID YOU KNOW?

And you thought biting your fingernails was bad? Some octopus in captivity have been known to eat their tentacles because of stress ... presumably caused by always having to work out how to open bottles to get at the food! Luckily for them, their limbs grow back later.

Meanwhile, back inside the shipwreck . . .

Leading off from the navigation room is an opening that leads downwards. Maybe there were once some stairs here.
You signal to Jack and float downwards into the black, watching out for the stinging tentacles of sea anemones which brush past your wet suit. There is a metal bulkhead door, slightly ajar, which you squeeze past. (The door is rusted fast and it doesn't open any further).

It is lighter ahead. Daylight! You push yourself out past some sponges and into the open. It's as if the ship has just been cut off . . . and finally you realise. This is not a small ship, just the front end of a much bigger one.

The SS Desdemona?

As you swim away from the wreck, the current pulls you North-East along the sandy sea bottom. In the dimness, you can make out other islands of life, where coral has formed over other pieces of wreckage. On one of these 'islands', soft coral sea fans wave on what looks like the broken-off bones of some gigantic ribcage.

Is it the skeleton of a whale?

Or . . . the timbers of a lifeboat?

You think you might be on to something here. You pull your knife out from its leg sheath and carefully scrape away at some of the growth encrusting one of the rib stumps. It crumbles away. It's definitely wood – perhaps this is all that remains of one of the ship's lifeboats. Pulling away some of the silt that has settled on the boat, a cloud billows up and blocks your vision. Scrabbling around, you lock onto something slightly bigger than your hand, so heavy that you are sure it contains metal but so covered in corrosion that it's unrecognisable. Whatever it is, it is covered in concretion. Using your knife, you scrape away some of the covering. The object looks like an old flare pistol. Jack is signalling to you that you have to start going up now. Before you return the pistol to its resting place, you have just enough time to uncover some writing stamped on the handle.

```
sdemona
erpool
gland
```

Here, at last, is evidence. You've found part of the ship, at least. But what happened to the rest? You didn't find the cabins with the safe that's reputed to hold the Fortune Star diamond. Think about what might have happened to the pieces of the ship after it broke itself in two on the coral reef. Lighter debris and the front of the ship may have been carried by the current, but the heavy mid-section probably just fell straight down.

Look at your undersea chart of Motorua on page 37.
Guess where that means you will be going?

Chapter 6
THE OPEN OCEAN

HEAVING YOURSELF OUT of the water onto your dive boat, you stop for a second and stare out to sea. It's pretty clear that the wreck of the SS Desdemona - at least the back half, which is the bit containing the safe with the Fortune Star diamond - is out there somewhere. You've checked the coral reef, the reef wall, and the ledge where you found the rest of the ship. It's now becoming increasingly obvious that you're going to have to start looking beyond the island of Motorua and its surrounding reefs.

BUT WHERE DO YOU START LOOKING?

The open ocean is vast! Nearly three-quarters of the Earth's surface is covered in ocean. And they are deep - up to eleven kilometres with underwater mountain ranges, deep ocean trenches, and masses of water that may have been scanned with sonar and mapped but has certainly never been explored. This is home to shoals of sleek tuna cruising at over thirty kilometres per hour, schools of dolphins, ten-metre-long Basking sharks, and whales that ply their way across the vastness in great migrations from one feeding ground to the next. And all this life is connected in thousands of food chains.

Tuna and dolphins eat fish, which in turn feed on smaller sea creatures. Whales sieve seawater through their mouths to collet tiny shrimps called krill.

And what's at the bottom of this whole web of life?

What do the whales and dolphins, tuna and sharks all rely on in the end?

PLANKTON!

Every living thing in the ocean is connected to plankton in some way. They either are it, they eat it, or they eat other animals that eat it.

What is plankton?

Basically, they are weenie little plants and animals that swarm in their millions in the oceans. Most of these creatures are actually no bigger than a pin head, but if you could put them all together, they would account for nine out of ten parts by weight of all the living things in the sea. Looked at another way; if you drained the sea and sieved it, you would be left with a heck of a lot of gunge, and you could only make out what the individual bits were made of, if you looked at it through a microscope. Sitting on top of that would be a slightly course slop of miniscule sea animals, like krill (little shrimpy things), that feed on the smaller plankton. On the very top, you would have the rest of the life of the sea - a heap of fish, whales, and everything else. There would be hardly any of those compared with the plankton and the krill. They would be like the cherry on top of a gungey, shrimpy cream cake.

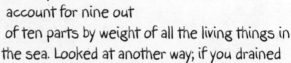

Here's a closer look at the animal plankton (also called zoo-plankton). Many, but not all, of the creatures that make up animal plankton will later grow into much more familiar sea creatures.

Can you guess what animals these larvae will grow into?

Match the letters with the numbers.

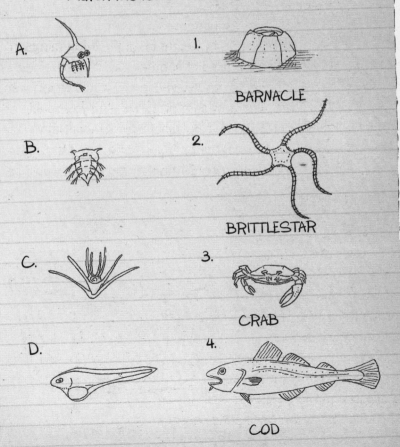

A.

1.
BARNACLE

B.

2.
BRITTLESTAR

C.

3.
CRAB

D.

4.
COD

Answers on page 64

ANSWERS from page 63

A. 3 – Crab   B. 1 – Barnacle

C. 2 – Brittlestar   D. 4 – Cod

Life is hard when you're zoo-plankton. They're not quite the bottom of the food chain, but pretty near to it, which makes them pretty expendable.

Take shrimp-like krill, for instance. In certain places in the Southern Ocean, where currents bring nutrients and plankton together, these swarm in their millions.

KRILL

Five centimetres long, at the whim of where the ocean currents want to take them, and look what they're up against...

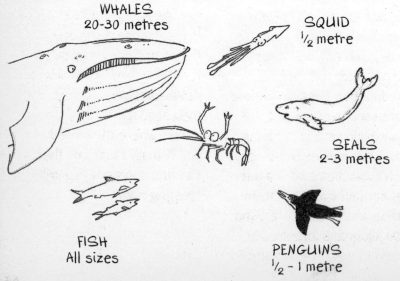

WHALES
20-30 metres

SQUID
1/2 metre

SEALS
2-3 metres

FISH
All sizes

PENGUINS
1/2 – 1 metre

The only consolation is that when a whale swallows them up, they'll have about ten million brothers, sisters, uncles, aunts, and other members of their immediate family with them!

DID YOU KNOW?

The biggest whales, such as **Blue whales** and **Right whales, eat krill.** Their mouths are like **huge filters** so that, after gulping in a mouthful of **krilly seawater,** they then **strain** it out through huge feathery-looking plank-like structures called baleen plates, which they have in the upper jaw instead of teeth. Finally, the whales swallow the soggy mass left behind. **Yum!**

It is not as hard as it might seem for a huge whale to fill up on such tiny creatures. In the nutrient-rich Southern Ocean around Antarctica, krill can swarm over several square kilometres in a living cloud, five metres or so deep. Each cubic metre of seawater may contain 63,000 of them. A Blue whale takes in around 1,000 kilograms (one tonne) of krill in each feeding and, in the few months before these cold seas ice over, the whales only need to feed four times a day. Having fed themselves up, they then head for warmer waters where they breed and virtually fast, until they can find another good krill-feasting spot.

USEFUL DIVING TIP

Diving with whales in the open ocean, to film them, for instance, could get rather cold. This is why you are likely to want a dry suit (yes, you can wear your undies and keep them dry). A hood is also a good idea here.

Although some people have managed to grip on to a whale's fin and be pulled along while it's swimming, is this such a good idea? Whales are huge and they are wild – even wilder, I would imagine, if some stupid diver is hanging on to their back fins. That tail can pack one heck of a whack – know what I mean?

A WHALE OF A QUIZ

Test your knowledge about whales and answer
True or False to the following questions . . .

1. Whales can breathe underwater, like fish.

2. The 'food chain' linking a Blue whale, plankton and krill would be: **krill** eaten by **plankton** eaten by **blue whale**.

3. Humpback whales 'sing'. These songs can carry for long distances. They do this to tell other groups of whales who they are and where they have been.

4. Fashion-conscious Victorian women used to use the baleen plates of whales to make stiff corsets to hold their dresses out.

5. Whales have their nostrils on top of their heads.

6. Dolphins are just small whales.

7. The hunting of whales has been banned by international law.

8. A Sperm whale's square head is shaped that way to hold its huge brain.

SPERM
WHALE

Answers on pages 68-69.

ANSWERS from page 67

1. **FALSE.** Whales are mammals, like humans. They have to come to the surface to breathe. Some, like Sperm whales, can hold their breath for more than half-an-hour. They shut down parts of their body they don't need whilst diving (like their digestive system), lower their body temperature, and slow down their hearts to last as long as possible before having to come back up to the surface for air.

2. **FALSE.** Plankton are eaten by krill that in turn are eaten by Blue whales.

3. **TRUE.** Scientists have recorded these songs and found out that every year they add a bit more to their songs. They say it is like the whale is passing on the story of where it has been and what's happened on that migration - a bit like your holiday snaps, but a musical version.

4. **TRUE.**

5. **TRUE.** When they come to the surface and blow a spout of water out of their blowhole, they are really just clearing their noses!

6. **TRUE**. So are porpoises and killer whales. The only difference, apart from the size, is that they are 'toothed' whales not 'baleen' whales, which means they have teeth for eating fish, not baleen plates for straining plankton.

7. **FALSE**. During the twentieth century, whalers have hunted and virtually wiped out many of the large whales for their fat blubber (used in the manufacture of lipsticks, amongst other things), and whale meat. Laws have been passed to prevent the killing of most types of whales **BUT** some countries are still allowed to do some whaling for 'scientific purposes'.

8. **False**. Most of that space is filled with a very pure oil which acts a bit like a Buoyancy Control Device. The whale is able to warm or cool this oil to change its density (heaviness), which allows it to float or sink.

DID YOU KNOW?

Not all whales eat just plankton or krill. Some of the baleen whales use their enormous mouths to gulp down whole shoals of fish at one time, and the toothed whales (like Sperm whales and dolphins), all hunt fish or other 'large' prey. Sperm whales can dive as deep as 1,700 metres. They like to hunt for giant squid . . .

For centuries, there have been mariners' legends about the **kraken** of the deep - sea monsters with huge tentacles - that were said to live in the deeper oceans, occasionally coming up to the surface to attract passing ships. Recently it has been proved that such creatures really DO exist.

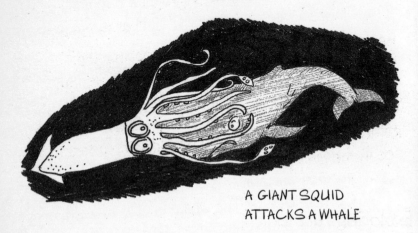

A GIANT SQUID
ATTACKS A WHALE

From time to time, the remains of large, unknown animals, presumed to be squid, have been hauled up in the nets of trawlers (fishing ships that drag a huge net behind them). Unfortunately, the change in pressure as their bodies reach the surface does rather unpleasant things and most have been brought up so rotten and half-eaten that it's difficult to tell with any certainty what they once were. Giant squid live so deep and are spread out so far and wide across the oceans, that no one has been able to study them properly yet. Still, this is what we do know.

Giant Squid . . .

- Are fifteen metres long or more (including tentacles).

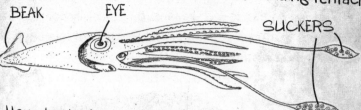

BEAK   EYE   SUCKERS

- Have tentacles with suckers for grabbing prey.
- Have beak-like mouth parts for biting chunks out of their prey – fish and other squid.
- Have huge eyes, the size of dinner plates, for gathering as much light as possible to help them see in the murky depths.

Exploring further . . .

How can you seriously hope to explore the vast ocean floor and find the wreck of the SS Desdemona? Flying over in an aeroplane isn't going to work, as you won't be able to see very far down into the water. Putting on a dry suit and diving down to look isn't an option. Even breathing special gas-air mixtures, you'll only manage a few hundred metres down and, besides, there's such a huge area to search.

How about using a deep-sea sub?

Fine – you might be able to go down a long way, but at that depth it's going to be so dark that locating half a sunken ship will be like finding a needle in a haystack, or should I say 'a drop in the ocean'. You need some way of scanning the ocean floor, finding the wreck, and then sending down the sub.

This is what you can use . . .

SONAR

It's the way that dolphins and some whales (such as Sperm whales) navigate in dark and murky water. You send out high-pitched sound waves and then time how long it takes for an echo to come back. If you know how fast sound travels underwater, you can accurately work out how far away the bottom of the ocean is. Of course, something above the sea floor, such as the solid remains of a ship sticking up, will echo back sooner.

With **modern sonar technology,** you can send down a **stream of sound waves to scan a wide area,** and then use a **computer** to build up a picture of what the ocean floor looks like. (Dolphins do very much the same thing, only they work it out in their heads).

This sort of technology isn't going to come cheap, and neither is the use of a mini-sub to search the wreck if you do locate the SS Desdemona. You ring your backers – the Jerry Steinburger Foundation – and they say 'No problem'. They'll stump up the costs. Finding the Fortune Star diamond is that important to them. All it takes is a chat with the oceanographic survey team who originally found the shipwreck on the shelf, and the equipment is ready to be used.

To get a more accurate scan, it helps if the **sonar device** is towed along fairly near to the **bottom**. In this case, you could use a surface ship to tow a **deep-sea sonar sled** just above the ocean floor, near to the reef edge.

But where do you want them to start their sonar sweep? Look at the undersea chart and decide the most likely place for the wreck of the SS Desdemona to be.

Here's a few hints . . .

The current along the reef wall flows North-East.

Lighter objects, like wooden lifeboats, would be swept furthest by the current.

Heavier objects would be more likely to just fall.

You know for certain that the rest of the ship's hull isn't in any place you've already been.

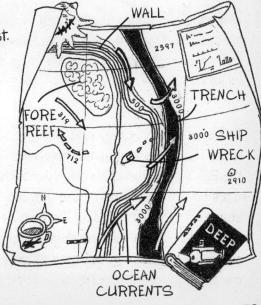

Got it!

The sonar sled locates a clear echo from some  object in the 'trench' at the bottom of the reef wall. That's the most likely spot to search. Just one thing! That's 3,000 metres down. That's going to take some diving to get to!

ABOVE: PART OF A '**SONAR SCAN**' (the back half of the ship's hull is shown in the middle).

Chapter 7
DOWN INTO THE DEEP ABYSS

YOUR JOB NOW is to get down to that possible wreck site that the sonar sled's scan showed. You need to check out if it really is the SS Desdemona and, if it is, get on with retrieving the Fortune Star diamond. You will be descending to the ocean depths, entering an environment where the equipment you will need is more like the stuff needed for going into outer space, than for any of the diving you've done so far!

What is it like down there?

If you could check on your dive gauge,
what readings do you think it would show?

1. Light level . . .

A. Light?

B. Meduim?

C. Dark?

3. Pressure . . .

A. Low?

B. High?

C. Extreme?

Answers on page 76

2. Temperature . . .

A. 0°C?

B. 3°C?

C. 10°C?

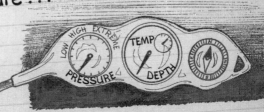

1. Light level: **Dark** – Pitch black in fact.

2. Temperature: **Above 0°C** (the water is not frozen.)

3. Pressure: **Extreme** – The pressure at eleven kilometres deep is 1,200 times the pressure that the air pushes on you – that's like having 12,000 kilograms pushing on each square centimetre of your body.

The first people to go down to the ocean depths were William Beebe and Otis Barton in 1931. They were lowered down in a hollow metal ball on the end of a very long cable, called a bathysphere. The ball had three thick windows and was only one-and-a-half metres wide. That had to fit two men, their telephone, lights, and apparatus to absorb the carbon dioxide they were breathing out (so that they didn't suffocate).

At one point, they nearly panicked. There was a pool of water on the floor. Had their craft sprung a leak? No. Any leak and a jet of pressurised water would have spurted though with enough  force to slice through them like a laser beam. The moisture was from their breath condensing on the cold walls of the bathysphere and dripping down.

The deepest Beebe and Barton reached in their bathysphere was 923 metres (3,028 feet). Beebe gave a commentary of what he could see through the porthole on the telephone. He described shoals of luminous fish that lit up the blackness like constellations of stars, gulper eels, and strange white fish that had no need for pigment in their skin. These are some of the things he saw...

RED SHRIMP

Beebe and Barton's deep sea 'monsters' are scary-looking, but less frightening when you realise how small they are.

The Gulper eel is twelve centimetres long, the viper fish is six centimetres long, and the hatchet fish is between one and six centimetres long.

GULPER EEL

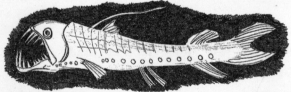

VIPER FISH

The sea serpent? That was over two metres long, but it turned out to be a bit of black rubber hose that had worked its way loose from the Bathysphere's hull.

DID YOU KNOW?

Hatchet fish have an amazing adaptation to stop themselves being seen from below. Special cells on their undersides glow exactly the same blue colour as the sea above, making them almost invisible to everything, except one particular fish which has evolved yellow lenses over its huge, round eyes (a bit like sunglasses), so it can see – and snap up – the not-so-invisible hatchet fish.

In the following years, technology moved on. People wanted to explore the ocean depths without being tied to the surface.

1931 – Bathysphere

1961 – Bathyscaph: THE TRIESTE

This was like an underwater airship. The tank on top was filled with petrol which was lighter than water but, being a liquid, did not compress (squash in). Bathyscaphs, like the Trieste, could float around the bottom of the ocean. One even reached to the very deepest part of the ocean called Challenger Deep, nearly 38,500 feet (roughly seven miles) down at the bottom of the Mindanao trench.

1965 – onwards – Deep Sea Submersible: ALVIN

There was even a flying saucer. Jacques Cousteau's Soucoup (French for 'saucer'), didn't dive as deep as the others but had precision controls for manoeuvring in places that regular divers couldn't get to.

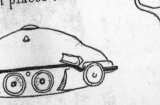

VENUS

A Gruesome Tale:
THE THRESHER

This is what happens if the pressure gets too great. In 1963, a brand new US Navy submarine was undergoing its sea trials before being put into active service. Its nuclear power plant developed a fault and the safety mechanisms did their job. They cut in – the reactor was shut off. Normally this would be fine but with no natural buoyancy and no power, the submarine started to

sink ... deeper and deeper. Its hull was designed to go down to a little over 300 metres. It reached that and carried on sinking.

Radio contact was lost...

Investigators, who searched for the wreckage using a towed submersible with special sonar sensors, said that the Thresher had imploded – that is, it had collapsed inwards. The pressure had been so enormous that it had squashed the hull completely in on itself. The metal plates at the rear of the hull had been the first to go. A wall of water had then cannoned forwards through the crew compartments, torpedo tubes, control and engine room. In under two seconds, the hull had been blown apart and the entire crew of 129 people were killed.

Life in the Abyss

What's all the fuss about? What's down there?

A surprising amount of life exists in the abyss considering how dark, cold and pressurised the environment is. Even at the bottom of the deepest ocean trench, submersibles like ALVIN and the Trieste found crabs, fish, and starfish. Most of these creatures rely on nutrients drifting down from the sunlit world above. There isn't much to be had, so the creatures are well spread out. Much of the deep ocean floor - called the Abyssal Plain - is like a desert. But in certain places where the continents meet, life abounds and here it is not the sun that provides the energy, but the heat of the earth itself.

Hydro-thermal Vents

Molten magma deep inside the Earth heats up water which then gushes up and out of cracks in the ocean bed. As it cools, the heated water deposits dissolves chemicals which build up into natural chimneys - black smokers or white smokers - depending

on the colour of the chemicals gushing out. Types of bacteria have evolved to feed on one of the dissolved chemicals, namely hydrogen sulphide - 'rotten egg' gas (it would be pretty pongy if you could put your nose out of your mini-sub and take a whiff of it). A whole eco-system has grown up surviving on this bacteria, and not just in one place - similar forms of life have been found wherever there are these hydro-thermal vents. This has led to theories that all life on Earth may have evolved originally in places like these. Think about it! Your great-great-great-great (several million times) grandparents may have been scummy slime living at the bottom of the ocean!

SUBMARINE HAZARDS

Imagine you're in a roving mini-sub. Apart from **the** Thresher, which was not a deep-sea vessel in any case, what can go wrong? All but two of the following events happened to the ALVIN deep-sea submersible. Guess which two are purely made up?

A. Impaled (spiked) when a swordfish attacked it?

B. Got too close to a hydro-thermal vent and its front window started to melt?

C. Toppled a black-smoker on itself?

D. Collided with another sub?

E. Became wrapped around by an octopus?

F. Became stuck down an ocean trench?

Answers on page 86
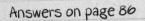

Kitting Out the Mini-Sub

This is the submersible that you'll be taking down the trench to search for the SS Desdemona. It is called the DESMOND, DEep SubMarine OceaN Diver.

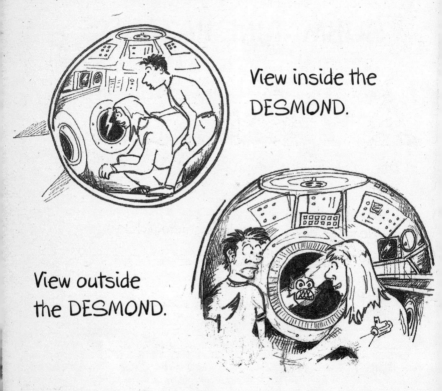

View inside the DESMOND.

View outside the DESMOND.

This is what you can expect the conditions to be like down there . . .

- Possible fast and unpredictable currents.

- Low visibility because of chemicals in the water.

- Enormous pressure.

The DESMOND has quite a number of extra fittings that can be added, depending on the job that needs to be done.

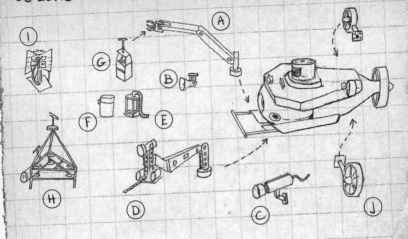

A. Remote-control manipulator arm to pick things up.

B. Spotlights to light the area.

C. TV camera to record a film.

D. Stereo camera – lets you make precise measurements of distance.

E. Vacuum sampler to suck up samples of mud and bacterial slime.

F. Specimen bucket to carry things picked up by the arm.

G. Mud grab – can grab and contain mud and soft rock samples and is operated by the manipulator arm

H. Acoustic velocity metre – measures the speed of water coming from hydro-thermal vents.

I. Water sampler for collecting water for testing.

J. Thrusters – for fine manoeuvring.

This amazing equipment will let you explore around the outside of the wreck, but you're going to want to go inside. According to the design plans of the SS Desdemona, there was a safe in the stateroom and that's where you're most likely to find the Fortune Star diamond. There's one remaining piece of kit that will let you go there, although you won't be going there 'in person'. You'll be taking the latest remote-controlled mini-robo-sub down with you. FRED (Free Roving Explorer (Deep)) will be your eyes and hands for delving into the black rooms and corridors of the long-sunken ship.

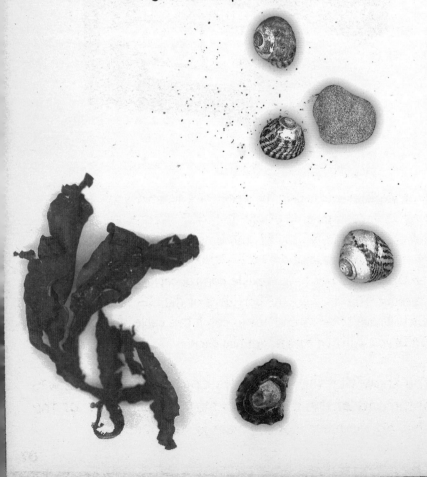

Chapter 8
THE TREASURE OF THE SS DESDEMONA

AS YOU BEGIN your descent of the deep ocean trench in the DESMOND, you make the final checks for your dive plan.

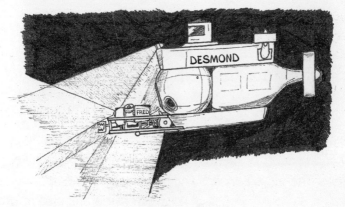

First, you'll have to locate the wreck and find a way in – some open door or crack in the hull – for FRED to enter. While you are going down, FRED will be safely housed in a framework 'garage' at the front of the DESMOND. FRED is connected to the DESMOND by a long, flexible control cable. While you are steering FRED through the corridors of the SS Desdemona, you will have to be careful not to catch this cable. If you lose FRED, you won't be able to get him back!

You know that the stateroom containing the safe was at the end of the corridor to the 'starboard' side of the ship, off the bottom of the main grand staircase.

This is a picture of how that staircase looked in 1903.

STARBOARD CORRIDOR. STATEROOM WITH SAFE AT END.

Remotely Operated Vehicles (ROVs)

These days, most deep-ocean exploration is done from the safety and comfort of the surface using remotely-controlled mini-subs. The sub's sensors and cameras give the operator a better view and idea of what is going on outside the sub, rather than by being inside looking out of the thick and tiny windows. And because it doesn't have to house a pressure compartment for a crew, this type of sub is much smaller and cheaper to operate. Using satellite link-ups and the Internet, remotely-operated vehicles can send information and be controlled from any part of the world. Who knows - pretty soon you'll be able to control a mini-sub using 'virtual reality' equipment or from your computer at home.

TITANIC

The most famous sea disaster of the last century has got to be that of the steam liner SS Titanic, which hit an iceberg and sank on its maiden voyage across the North Atlantic in 1912. For years, the location of the shipwreck remained a mystery. It was only in 1985 after extensive 'sweeps' with a sonar sled towed behind a search vessel that the ship was finally found. It was in two pieces, at a depth of 3,800 metres (12,460 feet), far too deep for divers. The submersible ALVIN was used to search the debris that had fallen from the ship on to the sea floor. A 'remote' mini-sub, called JASON JUNIOR, controlled from ALVIN, was used to explore inside the wreck itself.

Here are some of the things that were found in the wreckage of the Titanic. **Can you identify them?**

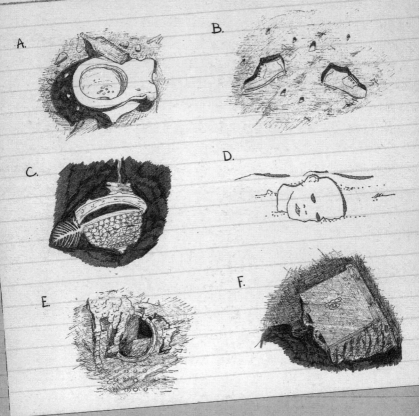

A.

B.

C.

D.

E.

F.

ANSWERS

A. Toilet   B. Shoes   C. Chandelier

D. A doll's head   E. Porthole   F. Safe

90

THE DESMOND descends . . .

DESMOND (holding FRED beneath it in a special tray) is released from its mother ship and starts the long descent down the trench. Before long, it is totally black outside, with the occasional pinprick of light shining out from the light-generating spots along the sides of some pilot fish that swim past. Other animals catch in the beam of your spotlights – dark red prawns and jellyfish, whose mushroom tops slowly pulse up and down. It is silent apart from the faint whirring of the sub's motors, the high-pitched beep-pause-beep of your sonar, and your breathing. The sonar shows the bottom approaching at 100 metres, 90, 80 . . .

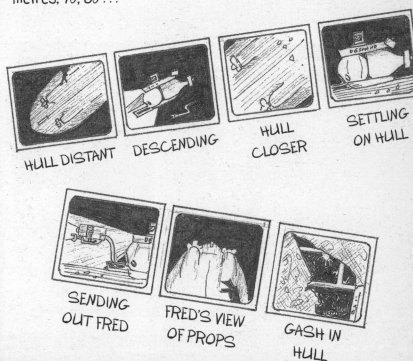

HULL DISTANT

DESCENDING

HULL CLOSER

SETTLING ON HULL

SENDING OUT FRED

FRED'S VIEW OF PROPS

GASH IN HULL

Although the hull is upside down, FRED is neutrally buoyant which means it doesn't float or sink. It's weightless in water. Using a joystick to control it from the pressure cabin of the DESMOND, you glide the robot sub around the rusty corridors and staterooms of the old liner.

You reach the grand staircase . . .

Which corridor will you take FRED down?

A, B, C or D?

Answer on page 94

You come to a room with the corroded remains of a safe in the corner. A white fish with pink eyes and a mean expression grudgingly moves out of the way as you pull at the safe's door with FRED's grabber arm, breaking off a chunk which you shine your light into.

Here's what you see...

Some fine white sediment swirls around in the water, undisturbed for nearly a hundred years. As the bits start to settle, something glints back in the beam of your spotlight.

A pile of gold bars and...

THE FORTUNE STAR DIAMOND!

ANSWER from page 92

A. Wrong. Remember, as the ship is upside down, everything will be back to front. That is the port (left) side corridor. Go back and try again.

B. Wrong. Some pinpoints of light you saw weren't the glinting reflection of the Fortune Star diamond, just some big-mouth fish that has too much liking for your TV camera. 'PFZZZ' – the screen blanks out. You are now flying blind!

C. Correct. Was that luck or did you have the sense to realise that if everything was upside down, the corridor would be opposite to where it was on the old picture?

D. Wrong. Remember the razor clams mentioned in chapter six? You just found some new deep-sea species of them. Or rather your link cable did. 'Pfzzz – BLIP'. There goes your screen as the connection with FRED is severed.

You stare at the picture on your monitor, zooming in until the gem fills the whole screen. Specks of sediment float across the image, but you can see that the diamond is flawless, perfect.

Before you think about getting it back to the surface, you remember the rules of underwater archaeology that require you to record and map out everything here before you remove anything. In such cold water, covered by silt, many things of historical interest will have survived and will need to be investigated.

That's for the archaeological teams that will undoubtedly follow this pioneering exploration dive that has taken you from the reef shallows, down the coral wall, and out into the open ocean.

What an achievement!

You've proved yourself as an expert underwater explorer. Now you've solved the mystery of the SS Desdemona and the Fortune Star diamond, fortune and glory await you. You'll be in all the papers, on the TV news, possibly even on a TV chat show too.

Everyone is sure to want to know how you did it. How did you go from simple skin-diving with just a snorkel, mask and fins to conquering a deep ocean trench with a submersible and a remote mini-sub?

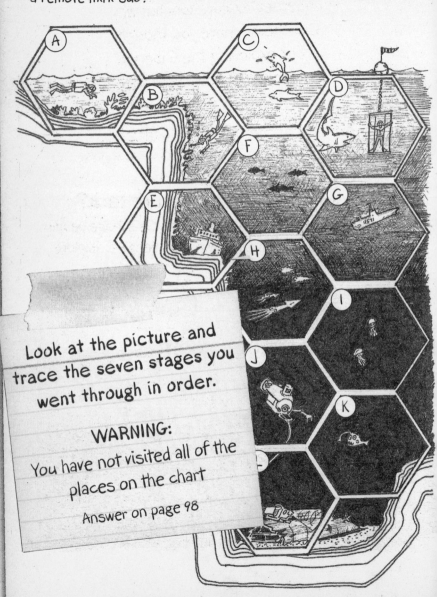

Look at the picture and trace the seven stages you went through in order.

WARNING:
You have not visited all of the places on the chart

Answer on page 98

You're now an expert at undersea exploration, but why stop there? Have you thought about exploring the Siberian wilderness? How about the savannahs of Africa, or the Amazon rainforest?

How will you get the treasure back?

Don't worry about that now. Leave that to the salvage people and go and find yourself some other challenge to explore.

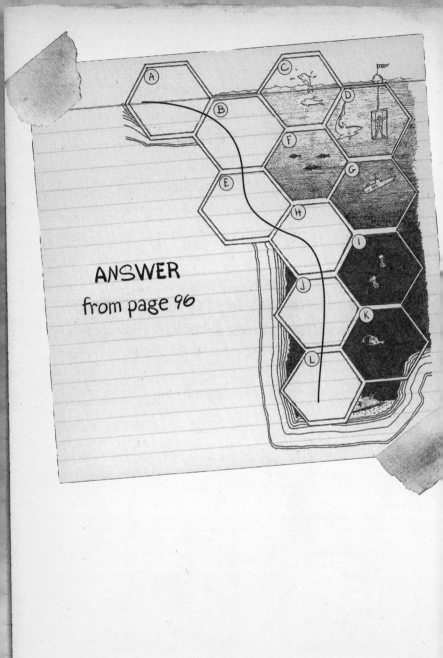

ANSWER
from page 96

EXPLORERS WANTED TO:

Trek through lion country

Motor across the teeming grasslands

Wander with wildebeest and zebras

Canoe hippo-filled lakes and
croc-infested swamps

Track elephants by the dampness
of their dung

Go in search of the legendary 'Smoke that Thunders'
and experience what it's really like to journey through
the hazardous African bush.

Simon Chapman

EXPLORERS
WANTED!

On Safari

SO ... YOU WANT TO BE A SAFARI EXPLORER?

Want to go to the African savannah where wild beasts roam ... ?

Do you want to meet ... **colourful** tribes ... ?

Find **ferocious** animals ... ?

Discover **wonders** of the **natural** world?
If the answer to any of these questions is **YES,**
then this is the book for you. Read on ...

THIS BOOK WILL give you the essential tips on how to travel through the African savannah, such as what to take and what you might find in the bush. **There are also some** pretty scary true-life stories of some of the people who have tried to explore it before ... so read on!

YOUR MISSION...

should you choose to accept it, is to mount an expedition through the African bush to find what the tribes of the interior know as the 'Mosai-aa-Tunya' — whatever that is!

The name translated roughly means 'The Smoke that Thunders'. It is said to be a magical place where the spirits live. No one has travelled there before, thought some of the nomadic Mkosi people, who herd cattle in the thorn-scrub beyond the great lake, say that on still days they can hear a deep rumbling sound and that clouds form over the Northern hills.

WHAT IS MOSAI-AA-TUNYA?

IS IT THE HOME OF SUPERNATURAL SPIRITS OR SOME FANTASTIC GEOLOGICAL PHENOMONEN?

This sketch map might help you — but only to a point. Once you have crossed the grasslands to the lake, you'll be travelling into the unknown.

You'll need to know how to survive the dangers you meet and how to make contact with the Mkosi, the only people who might be able to help you find

'THE SMOKE THAT THUNDERS'.

'The Smoke that Thunders'

Thorn-bush country

Swamps

Plains

N
W E
S

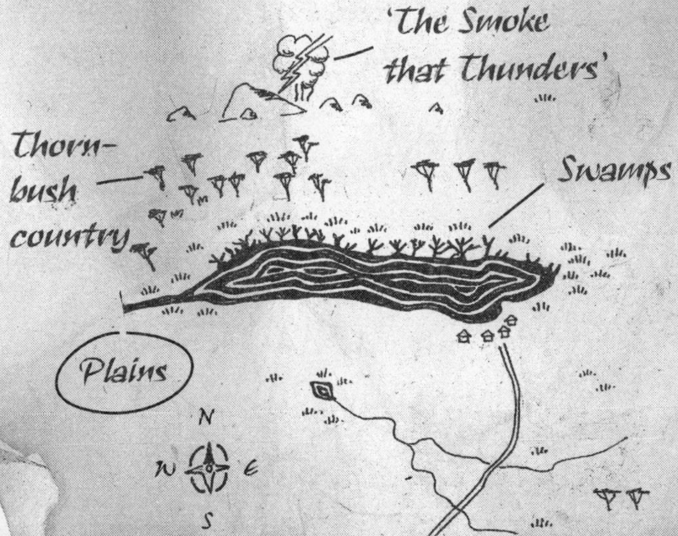

Time to set the scene . . .

Let's find out some vital facts about the savannah environment before the mission gets underway.

Well . . . It's a pretty big area. Most of Africa, in fact, stretching from Senegal in the West to Kenya in the East and down to South Africa. This is 'bush country'. You could drive for weeks on end and never get through it and just see grass and trees and rocky outcrops. It's a wilderness and you're going to explore it. But before you set off, you're going to need some extra information and you're going to need to know what to take. There are savannah grasslands in other parts of the world too. They have the same sort of climate and plants, but the animals are very different.

AFRICA FROM SPACE

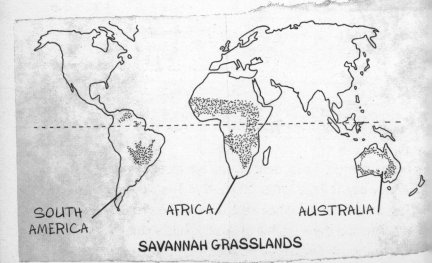

SOUTH AMERICA

AFRICA

AUSTRALIA

SAVANNAH GRASSLANDS

SOUTH AMERICA
Giant anteater
White-tailed deer
Rhea

AFRICA
Aardvark
Kob antelope
Ostrich

AUSTRALIA
Echidna (spiny anteater)
Grey kangaroo
Emu

But what's it like in bush country?

The first thing to understand about the savannah is that this is a place with a split personality.

Firstly, there's a DRY season. In fact, most of the year it's dry! Day-by-day, it gets hotter and hotter. The clouds disappear. The waterholes and the rivers dry up. The ground becomes cracked and the air is full of dust. Animals cluster anywhere where there's still a drop of water.

Fires start easily and can quickly ravage the grassland. But the roots survive and the grass will soon grow back once the rains come. All the life on the savannah - animals, plants, and people - are waiting for the clouds to return.

Then there's the RAINS - the other half of the split personality. The parched riverbeds are washed through with instant flash floods. Any low-lying land becomes soggy and swampy. The dead-looking grass suddenly bursts into life - and grows and grows.

This is the time of plenty, when the animals give birth to their young. There's more than enough fresh grass and leaves to go around for the plant eaters and there's more than enough plant eaters to go around for the meat eaters; the lions, hyenas, and hunting dogs. That means there's an awful lot of scraps and dead meat for the scavengers, and one heck of a lot of dung that needs clearing away! What happens to it?

What will you be travelling through?

Well, it's easier to get lost than you might imagine. Maybe not on the really open grassland, but in the bush, the scrub savannah, when you look around you will find that every direction looks the same!

VIEW FORWARD

VIEW BACKWARD

Just bushes ... scraggy-looking trees ... spiky mounds of mud?

The mud piles are termite mounds. They're concrete-hard, made from a mixture of chewed-up soil and termite spit . . . a lot of termite spit. Termites are tiny insects that live in huge colonies rather like ants. There'll be tens of thousands of them scuttling about inside in deep tunnels and chambers, walled in against predators and the hot sun, which would soon dry out their soft, white bodies. There'll be blind, eyeless workers, soldiers to protect them, a few male 'kings', and one

TERMITE MOUND

queen, the size of your little finger. She's unable to move; a podgy, bloated, egg-laying machine. And their food? Dead wood, leaves, and grass; and to make that go that little bit further, a special fungus that lives only on termite poo! As you can imagine, with that mixture it could get pretty smelly in there so termite towers have hollow tubes going up inside the outer layers that allows air to circulate. These shafts can go several metres under the ground and help to provide a controlled climate for the termites – a sort of insect air conditioning. There are a lot of these mounds around in the savannah; that means a stupendous number of termites and, in turn, a lot of plants to keep them going.

As you travel through the bush on your journey, it's worth remembering that it's the termites (and the ants too), not the antelopes, elephants, and zebras, that really shift the plant matter around here.

OK, it's fine admiring the insect architecture, but that's not going to get you through this scrub. You need a route you can walk along. How about a game trail? This is a path where large animals have bashed (and munched) their way through. There are tracks of antelope, and patches where the grass has been worn away by their hooves. There's a fair bit of dung too. And some of it's rolling!

ANTELOPE
TRACK

DID YOU KNOW?

Dung beetles stand on their front feet and roll dung with their back legs. They hide it, eat some of it, and lay their eggs in the rest. That's where their grubs grow up.

(How would you like to be raised in a ball of dung?)

You carry on following the game trail. There's something rustling behind the bushes ahead of you. It could be antelopes – or it could be the predators that eat them! (Remember, they also know that animals pass by here regularly). You creep up, making sure to stay downwind so that whatever is there doesn't smell you.

You are **downwind of the antelope but upwind of the buffalo. Bad move!**

What could be there?

An Impala . . . ?

A Giraffe . . . ?

A Lion . . . ?

It's a flock of goats and a small boy herding them.

Yes, people live here too!

Here's a savannah story about how to travel in style.

Bebe Bwana – 'lady boss' – set out on safari from Mombasa to Mount Kilimanjaro in East Africa in 1891. She hired lots of porters to carry all her stuff. This vital equipment included a long blonde wig and a silk ballgown, which she wore to impress the chiefs whose lands she was passing through. Forever keeping up appearances, May French Sheldon (which was her real name) did not walk cross-country on her expedition. She rode in a Palanquin (like a sedan chair or wheel-less carriage), which was carried by some of her porters. Sometimes, she slept in it. One night, she woke up to find something hitching a lift on top of it – a five-metre long python!

About the author

Writer and broadcaster, Simon Chapman, is a self-confessed jungle addict, making expeditions whenever he can. His travels have taken him to tropical forests all over the world, from Borneo and Irian Jaya to the Amazon.

The story of his search for a mythical Giant Ape in the Bolivian rainforest, *The Monster of the Madidi*, was published in 2001. He has also had numerous articles and illustrations published in magazines in Britain and the US, including *Wanderlust*, *BBC Wildlife* and *South American Explorer*, and has written and recorded for BBC Radio 4, and lectured on the organisation of jungle expeditions at the Royal Geographical Society, of which he is a fellow. When not exploring, Simon lives with his wife and his two young children in Lancaster, where he teaches physics in a high school.

CALLING ALL
EXPLORERS!

Win a free Explorers Wanted! badge by telling us what you think of this book.

There are four books in the Explorers Wanted! series in 2003, with exciting adventures and facts from every corner of the globe: from the hot and dusty African savannah to the freezing wastes of Siberia, from the insect-infested jungle to the deepest depths of the ocean.

We hope that you've enjoyed this Explorers Wanted! adventure. To help us make our next books even more exciting, we'd love to hear from you. We want you to tell us what you liked best about this book, and which places you think Explorers Wanted! should go in the future.

In return, we'll keep you informed about the series, author events that Simon Chapman might be involved in and, of course, fantastic competitions and give-aways.

The first 1,000 letters we receive will win a limited edition Explorers Wanted! badge to show off to their friends!

Send your ideas and comments to:

Simon Chapman
c/o Publicity Department
Egmont Books Limited
239 Kensington High Street
London
W8 6SA